The Good Spell Book

Collected and written by
Gillian Kemp

THE
GOOD SPELL
BOOK

LOVE CHARMS

MAGICAL CURES

AND

OTHER PRACTICAL

SORCERY

LITTLE, BROWN AND COMPANY

Boston New York London

To my father, Mike;
mother, Ruth, in spirit;
sisters, Lynette and Alison;
brother, Nigel;
my faithful Yorkshire terrier, Daisy May,
and her godmother, Katie Boyle.
To my agent, Chelsey,
publisher, Faith,
and to the one I love.
Thank you also to Peter Ingram
of the Romany Folklore Museum.

Contents

about the Romanies

The Aztecs, Homer's Greece, the England of King Arthur, and legions of other ancient cultures have long since vanished. But the Romanies — known in North America simply as Gypsies — survive, miraculously providing us a flesh-and-blood link with the roots of civilization.

This tribe of nomads, which originated in the Hindu Kush region of Kashmir and Afghanistan and began its wandering more than a millennium ago, first set foot in Western Europe six centuries ago. At once, they became objects of wonder, hatred, and controversy; they have remained so until the present day. Bringing with them the exotic traditions and dialects of far-flung cultures, they became known as skillful storytellers, musicians, and fortune-tellers. They were gifted and enthusiastic practitioners of palmistry, crystallomancy, and many other forms of divination, including Tarot card reading, which they claim to have introduced in Europe in 1427. In the Victorian era, they began traveling in gloriously ornate horse-drawn wagons, or caravans, known as *vardos,* which captured the public's imagination and inspired countless paintings, poems, novels, and children's stories. Though highly romanticized, the Romanies have always been widely mistrusted and persecuted for their ways. They eventually incorporated Christianity into their cultural traditions, and some became less conspicuous by adopting non-Gypsy names. Many became skilled tinsmiths, coppersmiths, and blacksmiths.

In the British Isles, society remains puzzled by the wanderers in its midst. Are they really a unique race of healers and clairvoyants? Or are they charlatans and parasites? Whatever the case, the

Romanies remain apart from the rest of us, indifferent to our electronic culture and clinging as best they can to age-old customs, courtship rites, and dialect.

Despite episodes of harsh persecution — including Hitler's extermination of a half-million Gypsies before and during the Second World War — Romany communities are still to be found the length and breadth of Europe and deep inside the former Soviet Union. In Britain today, barely a dozen families are to be found wandering the country in horse-drawn wagons. In a decade or so there may be none at all. If so, rural life will be much the poorer, for Romanies are true friends of the earth. With their nomadic existence they have lived closer to nature for longer than anyone else, and they are among the last free spirits on the face of the globe.

a few words of advice for amateur spellcasters

This bewitching collection of spells draws from the great cache of magical lore of the Romanies, supreme practitioners of divination and the mystic arts. The Romanies' common spells for attracting health and wealth, love and luck, are a treasure trove for all who believe.

All of these spells are simple and easy to follow, using everyday ingredients such as string, coins, paper, and candles. Even the more exotic requirements — Tarot cards, quartz crystals, and the recommended herbs and oils (such as rosemary, lemon, and sandalwood) — are now widely available.

Keep some Romany advice in mind while you work these spells:

By aligning your energies with the lunar cycle, and tapping into the natural tides and currents of life, you will increase the effectiveness and power of your spells. Because the moon turns the tide and our bodies are mainly composed of water, we wax and wane with the moon. Generally, psychic energy is highest when the moon is waxing (becoming full) and weakest when it is waning (diminishing in size).

When casting spells to attract someone or something into your life, tune in to the natural flow by working when the moon is waxing from new to full. The new moon is dark for three days before it appears as a crescent, and you should wait to work new moon spells until the crescent can be seen. For banishing-spells, to remove negativity and bad situations, you should work with the waning moon.

Remember, the most important ingredient of any spell is love. Thought and prayer are very powerful, and what makes the magic work is faith. Any spell you cast should come from the heart, and you should direct your thoughts like an arrow toward a target.

Many of the spells included here are fueled by candle flame, a practice that has its origin in fire worship. Romanies guard their fire carefully against wind and rain, not only for practical purposes of cooking and warmth, but because fire can be both a purifying agent and a destroying demon.

The minerals, herbs, flowers, and oils used in these spells also evoke nature's forces, and form a specific link from heaven to earth. Their subtle vibration brings results.

A few of these spells call for a crystal ball. In these cases you can use a magnifying glass instead, or a glass or metal bowl filled with water. If you're lucky, you may be able to find hollow, transparent glass floats used by deep-sea fishermen in antique shops. Crystal-gazers, known also as scryers, recommend keeping the globe clean. While using warm soapy water is fine, a solution of water and brandy, or simple running water, is preferred. Among Romanies the crystal ball is a sacred object, and they discourage the merely curious from handling it. If its energy appears to be dwindling, expose it to the waxing moon for three consecutive nights, concluding on the night of a full moon.

Do not be disillusioned if you feel that your spell has failed to work: it may only be your impatience which makes you doubt. Doubt is inverted faith, and nature cannot be rushed. Spells work in spirits' time. What is sent out mentally leaves an etheric trace, which adds power to the spell when repeated or reworded.

Again, faith in a spell intensifies the imagination and supports what is willed. Both words and thoughts are a powerful vibratory force. You must believe that what you wish for will come true.

Love

Romany lore includes a vast array
of powerful love spells. Collected here are time-honored
methods of bewitching a lover, bringing one closer,
and letting one down easy. The greater your passion when you cast
these spells, the better the results.

YOUR HEART'S DESIRE

You have met someone you desire. According to the Romanies this spell will ensure that he or she responds.

First, gather a fresh rose and two red candles, and find out the time of sunrise the next morning. Just before you go to sleep, place a red candle on each side of the rose.

The next morning at sunrise, take the rose outside or sit by an open window facing east, keeping the rose in front of you. Inhale the perfume and say aloud:

> This red rose is for true love.
> True love come to me.

Now go back indoors and put the rose in its original position. Light the candles, and imagine love burning in the heart of the one you long for. Keep the candles lit day and night until the rose fades. (If they are extinguished, the incantation will be broken.) When the rose is dead, pinch out the candles, and bury the rose.

[3]

TO WIN THE HEART
OF THE ONE
YOU LOVE

Write the name of the one you love on the base of an onion bulb. Plant it in earth in a new pot. Place the pot on a windowsill, preferably facing the direction in which your sweetheart lives.

Over the bulb, repeat the name of the one you desire morning and night until the bulb takes root, begins to shoot, and finally blooms.

Say the following incantation daily:

> May its roots grow,
> May its leaves grow,
> May its flowers grow,
> And as it does so
> [*Name of person*]'s love grow.

LOVE CHARM

Rosemary symbolizes remembrance. It is ruled by the sun and, according to the Romanies, is representative of people born under the zodiac sign Aries. So the following love charm is particularly effective on people born under the sign of the Ram.

In April or May, when rosemary is in season, choose pliable, willowy stems and bind them together into the shape of a heart. Form a mental image of the one you wish for. Then secure the rosemary heart with yellow ribbon, and if you have any threads from your partner's clothes or strands of hair, weave these in to create a stronger vibrational link. If your desired one is born under Aries, weave in a few strands of wool too.

Place the rosemary heart in a white envelope, and put it under your pillow. Before you sleep, repeat the words:

> Divine Love bless my sleep
> My true lover I shall keep.

The rosemary will dry with time and its life force will fade. When you feel your spell has brought the one you want closer, burn the heart in a fire, thinking while you do it of the flames of passion.

TO FIND A LOVER

On the day of a new moon, cut a red heart out of new red crepe paper or card. If you have a wild rose, use a fallen petal that is heart-shaped.

Take a clean sheet of white paper and with a pen no one else has used, write on it this incantation:

> As this red heart glows in candlelight,
> I draw you, lover, closer to me this night.

Then bathe and change into nightclothes.

When you're ready, light a red candle and read the spell aloud. Hold the heart in front of the flame and let the candlelight shine upon it.

Then place the heart and spell in a new envelope, and seal it with wax from the candle. Conceal the envelope and leave it undisturbed for one cycle of the moon, which is twenty-eight days from the day you began your spell.

By the time the moon is new, there should be new love in your life.

TO ATTRACT THE ONE
YOU LOVE

On a Friday evening, light a white votive candle and place it in a glass cup, or in a lantern. Imagine that the flame is a bright flame of love burning within your lover's heart, and that the lantern is your lover's torso.

As you stare into the flame, will the flame to rise. Your own passion will make it happen, and when it does, think of your emotions pouring into the flame. Think positively of your lover and draw him or her into the warmth of the candle flame as it rises and diminishes.

Say the following:

May this flame of passion burn within your heart.
From me, you will not part.

Leave the candle to burn itself out. Repeat the spell on consecutive nights until you receive the communication from your lover that you desire.

TO STRENGTHEN
ATTRACTION

If you love someone but sense he or she is not equally passionate about you, try this spell.

To attract their affection you need a few strands of their hair and a rose-scented incense cone or stick.

Light the incense and repeat the name of the one you long for several times, saying that you wish them to love you.

Hold the hair on the burning cone or incense until it frizzles away. As the hair burns, think of their indifference disappearing, and being replaced by passion.

Leave the cone or incense to burn out.

You can also try this alternative spell. First get a packet of seeds and a pot of soil in which to grow them. Then find a copper object that appeals to you — a penny will work. On a night when the moon is waxing, go outside and hold the penny in the moonlight. (The Romanies say that copper attracts love and that the magnetism of the moon will draw your sweetheart to you.)

Bury the penny in the soil in the pot, and carefully sprinkle the seeds on top to form the initial of your flame's name.

Love will grow as the seeds germinate, so keep the seeds watered and the pot in warmth and light.

Romany Love Formulas

Essential oils can be used in spells to generate a higher vibration. The following concoctions are used for anointing candles and for blessing objects. The formulas are not designed to be worn on the skin or used in bathwater.¶ When anointing a candle, drops of oil should be rubbed upward toward the top of the candle, which is regarded as the North Pole, and from the center toward the bottom, which is regarded as the South Pole. ¶ It is believed that your vibrations are transferred to the candle, making a spell more personal and more potent.

romance magnet oil

2 drops ylang ylang oil

2 drops sandalwood oil

2 drops clary sage oil

To attract love, rub Romance
Magnet Oil onto a pink candle and
then burn it for three hours
a day, every day, until the person
makes an advance. When used
for an existing relationship,
the ritual may be ended when
harmony is established or
resumed. If you have no one
special in mind, burn the candle
until a potential lover appears.
¶ The candle should be snuffed
rather than blown out,
the reason being that a spirit
resides in the flame and to
blow it out would blow your
prayer or wish away.

lover's oil

5 drops rosewood oil

5 drops rosemary oil

3 drops tangerine oil

3 drops lemon oil

Lover's Oil may be used to
enhance a relationship.
Consecrate a candle with Lover's
Oil and light it half an hour
before you have arranged for
your date to arrive.

marriage oil

2 drops frankincense oil

3 drops cypress oil

2 drops sandalwood oil

Marriage Oil is used to reinforce a marriage relationship, whether the union is good or floundering. It may also be applied to steer a relationship toward marriage. Simply burn a pink or lilac-colored candle sanctified with Marriage Oil when you and your partner are together.

desire oil

3 drops lavender oil

3 drops orange oil

1 drop lemon oil

Desire Oil is said to entice another to desire you. If someone already does, but needs a little encouragement, a red, orange, pink, blue, or white candle should be anointed and lit when the two of you are together.
¶ If you love someone and they are showing no response, speak their name as you light a candle blessed with Desire Oil. Allow the candle to burn for two hours before you snuff it out. Repeat the procedure every day until they react favorably.

Passing the Test

When Olive Rawlings, the last Romany girl in Britain to be born in a horse-drawn caravan, fell in love with a non-Gypsy, Dave Cox, he had to comply with centuries-old courtship rites and family tradition. Before Olive's family consented to their daughter's marriage in 1982, Dave had to travel with Olive's family for a year, to prove whether or not he could adjust and earn a living. ¶ His tests included carving pegs from hazelwood, and being able to build, drive, and repair a wagon and care for a horse and ride it bareback. Luckily, Dave proved a worthy husband. ¶ He and Olive went on to have two children, and bring them up as proper Romanies in their horse-drawn caravan.

TO GET A LOVER
TO CALL.

This spell is appropriate if you've had a lovers' tiff and you want your partner to make the first move toward a reconciliation. The spell is best begun when the moon is waxing, but if you cannot wait that long, begin weaving your spell regardless.

Take a photo of your lover and a photo of yourself. Using a paper clip or something similar, position the photos face to face, so that one image is literally on top of the other — the idea is that the person cannot see beyond your face.

[13]

Place the photos in the bottom of your underwear drawer and leave them there. The person you want should respond very quickly. Out of the blue, he or she will telephone, write, or reappear.

TO BIND
A LOVER TO YOU

For this spell you need a pack of Tarot cards. Separate the Major Arcana — the twenty-two cards that number 0 to 21.

From the Major Arcana extract the card that represents the astrological birth sign of the one you wish to bind to you. Also remove the card that represents your own zodiac sign. (If you share the same sign, you will need to make a photocopy of the card.)

[14]

ARIES
March 21—April 19 — The Emperor IV

TAURUS
April 20—May 20 — The Hierophant V

GEMINI
May 21—June 21 — The Lovers VI

CANCER
June 22—July 22 — The Chariot VII

LEO
July 23—August 22 — Strength XI

VIRGO
August 23—September 22 — The Hermit IX

LIBRA
September 23—October 23 — Justice VIII

SCORPIO
October 24—November 21 —— Death XIII

SAGITTARIUS
November 22—December 21 ——Temperance XIV

CAPRICORN
December 22—January 19 ——The Devil XV

AQUARIUS
January 20—February 18 ——The Star XVII

PISCES
February 19—March 20 ——The Moon XVIII

[15]

Simply take a hair from your lover's head, perhaps from his or her comb, and a hair of your own. Knot the hairs together with three knots. Place the strands between the two cards positioned face to face. The Romanies use a Gypsy peg — which looks like a hand-carved clothespin — but you could use a paper clip to secure the cards together.

Keep the cards in your purse, handbag, or briefcase, or wherever you are in frequent contact with them. When you feel the spell has worked, return the cards to the pack and burn the hair.

TO ENTICE LOVE

This spell can be used to attract love or to draw a lover closer. It should be begun on the night of a new moon.

[16]

Take a salt shaker and pepper shaker, and designate one the female and the other the male. Then take a piece of pink ribbon, and tie the female object to one end and the male object to the other, leaving about a foot of ribbon between them.

Every morning, untie the ribbon, move the objects a little closer together, and retie the knots.

Eventually the salt and pepper shakers will touch. Leave them bound together for seven days before untying them. By this time, love should have entered your life or your current partner should have drawn closer.

A lucky omen for love is to find a natural knot in the tendrils or shoots of a willow tree. The Romanies believe fairies tie the knots, and regard them as precious love amulets.

Such is their magic potency

TO HAVE YOUR LOVE
RETURNED

Use this spell when you've fallen for someone and want him or her to fall for you.

On a Friday, a day governed by Venus, light one pink, one blue, and one gold candle. Then place a horseshoe and a key on either side of the candles. (The horseshoe and key don't have to be real; they can even be the kind used for cake decorations.) The key represents the key to your heart, and the horseshoe luck in love.

Then take two roses, representing the pair of you. Wrap the flowers, the key, and the horseshoe in an item of clothing that belongs to your potential lover. If you don't have one, use a silk scarf that you've worn.

Place the items in a bedroom drawer and leave them undisturbed for fourteen days. It is a very promising sign if the roses appear fairly fresh when you remove them from the scarf. The petals should then be placed in a potpourri, or the roses buried. The horseshoe and key can be kept for luck.

that one placed under the pillow
of the person you desire is said
to bind you forever. To unknot one
would undo your luck.

TO ENCOURAGE
A LOVER'S RETURN

To bring a lover back all you need is a box of new pins, an onion, and the desire for your partner's love. As always, if your thoughts are vindictive, you will suffer.

Begin on a Friday night by pressing one pin into the onion. Imagine you are putting a thought into your lover's mind, and as you pierce the onion with the pin, say:

> It is not this onion I wish to stick,
> But your mind and heart I wish to prick.
> You'll think of me night and day,
> Until with words you arrive and say,
> "I Love You."

Leave the onion in sunlight, to invoke enlightenment.

This spell must be repeated for seven consecutive nights, preferably at the same time each evening. When the onion has seven pins in it your spell is completed. Plant the onion in the open with love's blessing.

TO BRING
A LOVER BACK

If your lover's attention has been wandering, the situation isn't hopeless. Try this simple spell.

Wait until Friday, because Friday is governed by the goddess Venus.

With your favorite pen and a piece of fresh white paper, write your first name and your lover's surname. Draw a square around them.

With your eyes closed say aloud:

[19]

> Our fate is sealed. We are one.

Cut the square out and place it inside your pillow-case, or among your most intimate possessions. Your lover will return.

LOVE
DIVINATIONS

To divine the initial of a future partner's first or last name, use this Romany saying that came into use after they adopted Christianity.

Take an apple and peel it without allowing the peel to break. Holding the peel in your right hand, say the following:

> Saint Simon and Saint Jude,
> On you I intrude,
> With this paring, to discover,
> The first letter of my own true lover.

Turn around three times in a counterclockwise direction before throwing the peel over your left shoulder. The peel is said to fall in the shape of your future lover's initial.

To find a length of red ribbon, red lace, red cord, or red wool is an omen of luck in love. If you should find such an omen, pick it up and while doing so, make a wish regarding the one you love

- Another custom is to hang the peel inside a door. The first person who enters will bear the same initial as your future partner.
- Another love divination using apples: Take an apple seed and give it the name of your lover. Place it in the embers of a fire. If it pops, the person loves you. If it burns silently, true love is absent.
- To see if a couple will marry, place two apple seeds together in the embers of a fire. If both seeds shoot off in the same direction, a marriage will take place. If the seeds part company, so will the couple in question. If both seeds burn in silence, the Romanies say, a proposal will never be heard.

[21]

If you have no one special in mind, finding red material signifies that new love will be making a dramatic appearance. Either way, it should be kept as a love amulet.

TO GET
A LOVING RESPONSE

Your partner's attention appears to be waning. He or she doesn't call as promised and doesn't appear to be making much effort to please you.

Take a photo of your partner and a quartz or glass crystal ball. If you have to, you can use a magnifying glass instead.

Place the crystal over the image of your partner's face and you will see the features magnified; the eyes and mouth appear to move and come to life.

Simply tell the person in the photo what it is you want them to do. According to the Romanies, he or she will get the message and respond.

[22]

TO RID YOURSELF
OF AN UNWANTED
LOVER

This spell is more complicated than most, but especially effective. Friday is the recommended day to work this spell.

First, light a new blue candle (blue being a healing color). Then ring a little bell three times.

On a clean white piece of paper draw a circle to represent the sun. Also draw a crescent moon, with the curved shape to the left, to represent the waning moon.

Stain the paper by squeezing onto it the juice from an apple. Fold the paper in half, then a quarter. Fold what you hold into half and a quarter again, imagining as you do so that you are folding up and containing the love you once shared.

Burn the paper in your candle flame and place the ashes on a clean white saucer. Dip your forefinger in the ashes and write the initial of your former lover on your forehead. Divide the remaining ashes into seven equal parts and evenly sprinkle them into seven pieces of clean white paper.

Fold the seven pieces of paper containing the ashes into seven little envelope shapes. Avoid spilling the ashes, because by doing so you will disperse the essence of the spell.

Pour a little candle wax over the seal of each parcel. It is most important to think loving thoughts about your partner as you do so.

Bury each parcel with love in your garden.

TO RID YOURSELF
OF A PERSISTENT AND
UNWANTED LOVER

For this spell you need an item of your former lover's clothing.

From the material, cut a square large enough to write his or her name on. On the night of a full moon, light a pink candle. Write your admirer's name on the cloth. (Chalk works particularly well.)

Wishing your suitor well, burn the name on the material in the candle flame while saying:

> This light will burn out any flames of passion
> [*name of person*] has for me.
> He [or she] is gone, I am free.

Leave the candle to burn down until it extinguishes itself.

To conclude the spell, the candle stub should be burned, or buried in the remains of the clothing from which you cut the square.

Marriage Folklore

If a courting Romany presented his neck-scarf
to his girlfriend, and she wore it constantly,
it was a sign that she loved him.
Such a gesture might incite him to propose.

Romany folklore says
that you will be rich in love and wealth if
you marry at the time of a full moon.
A couple can expect more prosperity by
marrying when the moon is waxing rather
than when it is waning.

According to Romany folklore it is unlucky
to present a married couple with a gift of a knife.
It symbolizes that their love will be cut in two.
The gift of scissors and any other
cutting implements bodes misfortune as well.
However, the recipient can counteract the
impending doom by giving a coin to the person
presenting the sharp object.

It is also a sign of misfortune
if the bridegroom looks
over his shoulder as his bride
approaches during the
wedding ceremony. The Romanies
say it symbolizes that he will
always look behind him in regret.

For love, luck, health, and prosperity,
the Romanies believed in breaking bread
over the heads of the bride and groom.
The bread was made by mixing flour with fresh or
dried fruits combined with a little blood taken
from the ring fingers of the couple.

One marriage custom that continues to be
observed is the belief that it is unlucky
to marry in Lent:

Marry in Lent and you will live to repent.

Monday for wealth,
Tuesday for health,
Wednesday the best of all,
Thursday for losses,
Friday for crosses,
And Saturday, no luck at all.

According to Romany folklore,
if the surnames of a couple who plan to marry
begin with the same initial, it does not bode well.
They say, "If you change the name but not the letter,
you marry for worse and not for better."

Another belief is that
the first of a couple to fall asleep
on the wedding night will be
the first to die.

THE ETERNAL
TRIANGLE

If you are undecided between two admirers, magic can help.

Take two tulip bulbs. With a new pin scratch the name of one suitor on each bulb. Remembering which bulb represents which lover, plant the bulbs beside each other in a pot, window box, or garden.

The bulb that blooms first will reveal the admirer who is most deserving of you.

[29]

To solve a couple's problem,
go to a river with a shoe
belonging to the missing partner.
Write your wish upon the shoe,
and toss it downstream.
The problem will flow away.

TO AVOID DIVORCE

Divorce is taboo among the Romanies, so this spell is used to heal a broken marriage. It requires little more than an apple, true love, and the sheer determination to keep the marriage intact.

The advantage of this spell is that a link has already been established. The marriage simply needs reinforcement or bridging.

Buy a perfect-looking apple. If it is summer or autumn, pluck an apple yourself; an apple right off the tree has more life force in it.

Cut the apple in half. Regard it as an auspicious omen if the seeds have not been severed with the knife, but don't worry if they have.

On a piece of clean, unused white paper write the woman's full name. Next to it, write the man's.

Cut out the names, keeping the piece of paper they are on small enough to fit between the apple halves. Then place the paper with the names between the two halves and imagine the marriage being healed.

Skewer the apple halves together with two pins, inserting the pins diagonally from right to left and from left to right.

When you position the pins send your love to your partner and ask for the love to be reciprocated.

Romanies use their campfire to bake the apple. You could place your apple in your hearth or in the oven instead, and bake until the apple appears whole. If you can get your partner to eat some of the cooked apple, so much the better.

UNWANTED
DIVORCE

When an unwanted divorce appears likely, the Romanies advise the friend who wants their partner to return to light a purple candle.

Pierce it with a pin from right to left, so that the pin tip emerges on the left side of the candle. Then take a pin with a blue head and pierce the candle from left to right. As you do so, focus on the point of the pin, and the idea of crossing the other person's path. Leave the candle to burn and extinguish itself. Afterward, bury the pins.

NETHER GARMENT SPELL
FOR FIDELITY

Although in Romany culture divorce is taboo, their marriages are not necessarily happier than most, and sometimes partners do go astray. But there is a spell that draws a partner home to his or her original ties. This spell is very basic, as down-to-earth as the Romanies themselves. It gets to the point and apparently works.

Choose a pair of your partner's underwear and a pair of your own. Take two nutmegs, and write your partner's full name on one and your own on the other. Bind the two nutmegs with a red cord (to symbolize passion). Wrap them in the underwear, and place them in a clean white envelope. Sleep with them under your pillow if your partner is away, or embed them in a drawer where you keep your favorite or most sensual clothes.

[33]

TO COMMUNICATE
WITH
AN ABSENT PARTNER

First, light a pink candle. Now, holding a photo that clearly shows your partner's face, look into his or her eyes. You can look deeper into the eyes and beyond, into the mind, by placing a crystal ball or a magnifying glass on top of the image.

Speak directly to the photo or through the object you have chosen to magnify it with. The eyes, mouth, and facial features in the image will move in such a way that it appears you are speaking directly, face to face, to the person you're trying to contact. At this point you have made the connection.

Tell the person what it is you want, or ask a question. The response will come to you telepathically.

Blow out the candle and wave the photo through its smoke from north to south and from west to east. Return the photo to where you normally keep it.

Health

The independent Romanies, after hundreds
of years of wandering, had to be their own doctors.
They learned how to use herbs, plants, and
other remedies to cure them when
they were sick or injured. ¶ They strongly believe
that many illnesses are affected by the mind.
Thinking you are healthy can actually make you fit.
A Romany mother who says to a child,
"Let me kiss it better," can actually make the child
better by giving them faith.
The Romanies also say that sending love to a
sick person — whether the person is aware of it or not —
can improve that individual's condition.

CURING
DEPRESSION

The Romany philosophy is that depression attracts depression like a vibration. To ward it off play happy music or mix with happy people. Alternatively, walk to a hilltop to literally rise above your problem. Looking down on roads, cars, houses, and people makes them appear in better perspective.

Romanies always try to look on the bright side of any situation. However, if that is not so easy, try this Romany antidote to the blues.

[37]

Peel several cloves of garlic and place them in a saucer. Pour white vinegar over the cloves until they are partly immersed in it. Place the saucer beside your bed while you sleep. The garlic is said to turn pink because of the negative energy it absorbs.

The cloves should be buried in the morning and replaced by fresh cloves at night.

DIETING

This spell makes it amazingly easy to stop eating sweets.

Take a piece of cake, a cookie, or a chunk of chocolate — whichever sweet you're trying to banish from your life — and bury it in a pot or in the garden.

Plant three cloves of garlic on top. The cloves will purge you of your craving by the time the garlic has grown.

[38]

TO CURE
A BAD HABIT

To help yourself or another to give up smoking, nail biting, or any other unwanted habit, first find nine strands of hair belonging to the afflicted person, and wind them around an iron nail. The nail should then be hammered into a wooden post. The habit is believed to abate as the nail rusts.

TO CONCEIVE
A SON

At your most fertile time of the month, place one red rose in a vase on a table. Light a red candle, which is symbolic of Mars, ruler of vigor and vitality. Next, light a green candle. This color is associated with Venus, love, and harmony. Place it to the right of the red candle. Place a yellow candle, to represent the sun, above the red and the green candles to form a triangle. The number three represents the male reproductive organs, and sexual force.

On a bay leaf — because bay is ruled by the sun — write the phrase "I wish to conceive a son." Place it face up between the candles.

Now close your eyes and imagine a red rosebud in your womb. Visualize the rosebud unfolding and coming into bloom.

Open your eyes and visualize the candlelight being channeled into your womb, then close your eyes and continue with the visualization for as long as you can.

Leave the candles to burn themselves out. Take the bay leaf, kiss it three times, and place it under your pillow, where it should stay throughout your fertile phase.

All that is required now is the cooperation of your partner.

TO CONCEIVE
A DAUGHTER

You need to prepare and work this spell when you are reaching your most fertile time of the month.

The idea is to make a doll that resembles you as closely as possible. Take some modeling clay and mold it into the form of a pregnant woman; press hair from your comb into her head, dress her in clothes like yours, even cut out a photo of your face and place it on hers.

When the doll is prepared, place her on a bed of fresh lavender or on a pink scarf sprinkled with lavender oil. (Lavender is a masculine flower, as its shape dictates, and it attracts love.) Take her to a table in a room without electric lights, and light a pink candle to the right of her.

Using clean, white paper write the phrase "I wish to conceive a daughter." Place the paper beneath the lavender or scarf.

If you feel ill, before going to b
simply say: "I want to be healed
while I sleep." Spirits will heal yo
overnight and you will wake
feeling better than usual.

By following advice given in s

Fold the paper around the doll on her bed and tie a yellow ribbon or cord around her. Place your doll beside your pillow, or on a bedside table, with a piece of quartz crystal and a moonstone. Quartz is sometimes called "sacred fire" because it intensifies the rays and energy of the sun, a masculine force. Moonstone, governed by the moon, is a feminine, emotional stone. Its nature and aura improve health and reveal the future. Like females, it changes with the moon: it transmits energy to health when the moon is waxing and gives power to desires when the moon is waning.

Your partner's desire completes the spell and brings it to fruition.

many people have been
miraculously recovered.
(This form of divination is called
iatromancy.)

PREDICTING
THE SEX OF A BABY

To determine whether an expected baby will be a girl or a boy you must find a location where red and white roses grow together.

The pregnant woman, with her eyes closed, should be guided to the rosebushes. She should then walk seven times in a counterclockwise circle before heading, still with her eyes shut, toward the roses.

[42]

If the rose she picks is white, a daughter will be born; if red, a son.

A more well-known method is to dowse with a pendulum. Instead of an actual pendulum you can also use a ring suspended from a length of string or human hair. The pendulum, as it is held over the mother's stomach, should be asked to swing in a clockwise circle if the baby is a boy and in a counterclockwise circle if it is a girl.

TO REMOVE WARTS

There are a number of methods used by the Romanies to remove warts.

- Rub the wart with a stone, then place the stone in a tissue or handkerchief. Give the stone in the handkerchief to a friend to bury at a crossroads. The wart will wither as the handkerchief decays.
- Another method is to rub the wart with a potato instead of a stone. No handkerchief is required for this cure; simply bury the potato, and the wart will disintegrate along with the potato.
- Someone's wart can be bought for a penny. The person selling the wart should place the coin between two halves of a potato, which the buyer buries for them.
- An alternative, which can remove several warts at a time: rub each wart with chalk and then use the chalk to draw a cross on the back of a fireplace. The warts are said to disappear gradually as soot covers the chalk marks.
- To charm warts away, use a piece of string: tie as many knots as there are warts, then bury the string. The warts will decay along with the string.
- Yet another method: take a pin and point it at the wart, without touching it. Tell the wart that it will be gone. Then stick the pin in turf or soil. The wart withers as the pin rusts.

[43]

SYMPATHETIC
SORCERY
FOR·ILL HEALTH

According to the Romanies, there is no simpler way to cleanse someone of an illness than to cut their fingernails and trim their hair. The nail and hair clippings should then be buried. Some say throwing the clippings into a stream, river, or running water will wash the illness away.

[44]

The curse of ill luck that a single magpie flying from right to left is said to bring may be neutralized by saying:

"Good morning, Mr. Magpie, how's your wife?"

If it is after midday, to avert misfortune you can bo

ANOTHER WAY
TO ALLEVIATE
ILLNESS

Take a coin you have found on the ground and put a pinch of salt on it. Then transfer the salt into a small amount of boiling water, and let it dissolve. When the water has cooled, use the coin to flick the saline solution onto the palms of the patient's hands and on the soles of his or her feet.

Yet another traditional remedy uses candle magic. On a blue candle, use a pin to inscribe — moving from the base to the tip — the name of the person who is ill. Pierce the candle with the pin and leave it there. Let the candle burn down and extinguish itself, and keep the pin for future spells.

[45]

to the bird and say:
"Good day, Your Lordship."

PROTECTION SPELL

This spell can be used to improve the health of an elderly person as well as to keep harm away from someone who is housebound.

Take a horseshoe or an iron nail and bless it by immersing it in salty water. Bury it in the garden of the sick person or in a potted plant. Leave the tip poking out of the earth, to act as a conductor to disperse the energy. Say when you bury it:

> Ill health I do tell,
> Run through this iron,
> [*Name of person*] is free and well.

Sneezing

"*Coughs and sneezes spread diseases*" —
and according to the Romanies,
sneezing is more than a sign of a cold.

Sneeze on a **MONDAY** you'll escape danger,

Sneeze on a **TUESDAY** a kiss from a stranger.

Sneeze on a **WEDNESDAY** a good news letter,

Sneeze on a **THURSDAY** a gift which is better.

Sneeze on a **FRIDAY** news will cause sorrow,

Sneeze on a **SATURDAY** you'll travel tomorrow.

Sneeze on a **SUNDAY** ask God to bless you

All the week, your health to keep.

TO EASE
LINGERING ILL HEALTH

This spell was traditionally used by mothers to cure their children.

Go to a stream with an empty jar, and let the current fill it. Take the jar home, and add seven cloves of garlic and seven pieces of coal. Leave it to steep for seven days. Meanwhile, find a three-forked twig.

Boil the contents of the jar and stir it with the twig. When the water has cooled, flick it seven times on the patient. This is believed to avert the "evil eye," a spirit of misfortune.

[49]

It is also thought that illness can be washed away by going to a stream on a new or full moon to rinse the sick person's hands and face.

TO INCREASE
HEALTH AND VITALITY

A quartz crystal emits a frequency of energy, a vibration. Romanies are known for using crystal balls for clairvoyance, but they also use quartz rock crystal for healing.

If you have a piece of quartz, first wash it in warm soapy water and rinse it with running water. Then hold the crystal in both hands. Close your eyes and imagine being bathed in white light. Visualize the area of your illness and point the crystal to that site. Imagine a stream of light flowing from the crystal and bathing the area in its pure rays.

Place your crystal under your pillow while you sleep.

[50]

If a Romany has a nosebleed,
he allows a few drops of blood
to fall on the earth.
The drops are then covered with soil

TO REMOVE
A HEADACHE

To remove a headache, rub your forehead with a stone and then cover the stone with soil. The ache is said to be absorbed by the soil.

- Alternatively, you can rub a headache away by rubbing a horseshoe on your forehead. (A piece of iron is said to work just as well.)
- Yet another method is to lie down and place a quartz crystal on your pillow. If you can't lie down, try holding a quartz to your head for a few minutes to relieve the symptom.

[51]

so that earth spirits
can work their healing.

TO CURE BALDNESS

A Romany remedy said to make hair grow on a balding patch is to mix equal measures of rosemary oil, almond oil, and bay rum and to rub that into the scalp morning and night.

To halt thinning, rub garlic oil into the scalp morning and night.

To strengthen hair and prevent loss, rinse with an infusion of half a teaspoon of rosemary sprigs in one cup of water.

To grow a good head of hair, Romanies say:

Of weak thinning hair you will never complain,
If you cut your hair in the moon's wax
And never in her wane.

To stir food or drink with a knife is "to stir strife."

TO EASE CRAMPS

The Romanies say that sleeping with a bowl of water from a stream or spring under the bed relieves cramps.

Another remedy is to thread corks on a red cord, or wrap them in a red silk scarf, and place them at the foot of the bed.

[53]

TO LOWER A FEVER

To lower a fever use a simple salt spell. Throw a handful of salt into the flames of a fire — salt turns the flames blue. Look into these blue flames, and visualize the patient well again. As you do so say the words

Fever burn, good health return.

BAD BREATH

The Romany remedy for bad breath is to eat at least one fresh, raw apple every night before going to bed. Another antidote is to chew parsley, peppermint, fennel, or caraway seeds.

[54]

A BUMP
ON THE HEAD

When a child bumps its head, press the flat side of a broad-bladed knife against the bump to alleviate swelling. Then thrust the knife into the earth seven times, so that the pain is transferred from the child to the ground.

FOR SIGHT
AND INSIGHT

To improve eyesight and clairvoyant vision, boil a little spring water with a pinch of saffron on a Sunday. Romanies say a saffron bath not only increases clairvoyant vision, it instantly soothes painful eyes. Saffron is ruled by the sun sign, and dedicated to magic and love because of its yellow color.

Another method to relieve sore eyes is to put gold rings in the ears. (Perhaps this is why so many Romany children as well as adults have pierced ears.)

[55]

Hair removed from a brush or comb should be buried or burned.
It is believed that if a magpie builds a nest with it,
the hair's owner will meet an untimely death.

HEALING FROM AFAR

To heal someone who is not nearby, you need a feather, rosemary oil, a shell, a stone, an onion, and a horseshoe (if you have one).

Write the name of the person you wish to heal on the onion (a ballpoint pen or a pencil works well).

Plant the onion bulb in a pot or garden, and put a stone to the north, three drops of rosemary oil to the south, a shell to the west, and a feather to the east. Cover the objects with soil.

Place the pot on a horseshoe, or place a horseshoe close by if the bulb is planted in the garden. This spell uses the strength of Mars, the god of war — both the onion and the horse are governed by Mars — to win the battle over the illness.

[56]

Pets

The Romanies strongly believe in the power of hands-on healing for dogs, horses, and smaller pets such as cats, rabbits, guinea pigs, hamsters, mice, and birds. ¶ These remedies are not an alternative to visiting a vet. But they may be used in conjunction with veterinary treatment, before or after surgery, or simply if your pet appears to be "under the weather."

TO HEAL
A CAT WOUND

To heal a cat after it's been in a fight, the Romanies recommend that you first light a blue candle. Place your cat on your lap or let the cat find its own comfortable place to lie. Soothe it with loving strokes until it purrs or appears relaxed and comfortable enough to stay put for five or ten minutes.

Close your eyes and pray for a spirit vet to work through your hands. After a few minutes you should feel heat emanating from your palms. You may then feel your hands being guided to various parts of your cat's body. Direct them to where they are drawn.

Imagine the colors of the rainbow — red, orange, yellow, green, blue, purple — streaming into the cat.

Finish by thanking the spirit vet who used your hands to channel healing energy. Then say,

Kitten scrap scrabble scrap

before giving your cat a kiss to seal the spell.

DOG HEALING

Place your dog in a comfortable position or let it find its own spot in which to lie down.

Sit beside your dog and pray for a circle of gold light to be placed around you both for protection, and for a circle of blue light to be placed around you and your dog for healing. Then say the Lord's Prayer.

Place your hands palms down over your pet.

Visualize yellow light, then blue, green, indigo, and violet rays permeating your hands and then passing into your pet's body.

End by asking for a cloak of spiritual protection to be placed around your pet to protect and keep it from harm.

This can be repeated several times a day.

Cat Lore

Cats have been revered as magical since the time of the ancient Egyptians. A cat washing itself is believed to be a forecast of rain. To see it wash behind its ears is a sign that a visitor will call. If it sits with its back to the fire, it is a sure sign of frost.¶ Your cat may also assist divination. Leave a door open and think of a question that can be answered yes or no. Call your cat into the room and notice which paw it first places on the floor. If it is the right forepaw, the answer is yes; if the cat steps with the left, the answer is no.

Horse Whispering

Horse whispering is shrouded in mystery.
It is an inexplicable method employed by the Romanies to tame wild and temperamental horses.¶ Tradition says the secret to horse whispering was granted as a deathbed legacy from a horse charmer to his eldest son. The Romanies say that one who has received the gift of horse whispering cannot die peacefully until he or she has passed on the talent.¶ There are tales of horse whisperers meeting secretively in moonlight to practice their equestrian skills and to discuss hypnotic, herbal, and magical formulas.¶ Some believe horse charming is the application of herbs or aniseed to the horse's nose or bridle or the recitation of the Lord's Prayer in its right ear. Whatever it is, it is a secret the Romanies guard jealously.¶ One spell they do share is said to make the horse fearless of commotion and also of supernatural beings. The charmer first draws a circle on the left front hoof with a piece of coal and a cross on the right front hoof. Then the charmer spits on a piece of salted bread and feeds the bread to the horse.

TO CALL
A STRAYING PET

When a cat, dog, or other pet has gone missing, do not despair. Pets are tuned in psychically to their owners and will respond to an invisible call even at a distance.

Place some food and milk or water in the pet's familiar bowls. Light a blue candle next to them and say:

My fair beauty gone astray
Please come back to me today.
With my yearning heart and wonder,
Please come back to me from yonder.

Afterward leave the candle to burn down, or snuff it out when your pet returns.

[63]

TO DETER STRAYING

To deter a pet from straying, dig a hole and then fill it with salt, charcoal, and fur from your pet's brush or comb.

Another custom said to prevent straying is to cut out a piece of soil bearing the animal's footprint. The soil should then be placed under a strong tree in your garden (willow is preferable). Alternatively, keep the print indoors in a plant pot or dish.

Another well-known means of preventing a cat or dog from leaving home, particularly after a house move, is to rub its four paws with butter.

[64]

TO FIND A MISSING
CAGED PET

A bird, hamster, guinea pig, or rabbit that has gone astray can be welcomed home with this basic spell.

Call the pet's name three times. Tie a yellow cord around its cage, after having replenished its food and bedding.

Then call the pet's name three times again.

[65]

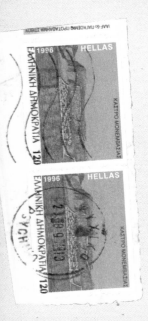

PET SAFETY SPELL

When your pet is away at a kennel or at the vet's, you can strengthen your psychic link with it and ensure its safe and happy return. Place a blue ribbon or cord in a circle around its bed, favorite chair, or toys, and tie a knot to form a circle. Unknot the cord only when your pet is back in your safekeeping.

[66]

Wealth

The Romanies' motto is:
"Think lucky and you'll be lucky." ¶ Formerly, many Romanies
were wealthy people, and some still are.
Their belief is that possessions should only be procured in
harmony with what is right and good. Simply put,
they believe good is creative and evil destructive. ¶ For the
majority of Gypsies, their caravan — their *vardo*, or wagon —
was their most treasured possession.
However, much of their working, living, and cooking
was carried on outside, where they were in touch with
the elements. They believe that the body is
a vehicle for the spirit on earth, and the *vardo* is a vehicle
for the body on earth. ¶ According to Romany custom,
when the occupant died, the caravan and most
of its contents were burned to ashes.

ESSENTIAL
MONEY SPELL

Around campfires or in their sunny *vardos* the Romanies invoked spells to bring prosperity. The following spell has been popular for centuries; in the past, coins of an earlier date were used, preferably gold.

Take five short green candles and ten quarters. Rinse the coins in warm salt water. Set five saucers in a circle and place one coin in the center of each saucer.

With a little melted wax, securely fix a lighted candle on top of each coin. Distribute the five remaining coins inside the circle so that they form a five-pointed star with the apex facing away from you.

Say aloud:

I need [*amount of money*] immediately.

Imagine green and purple five-pointed starlight glowing from the candle flames. Imagine coins cascading from the flames for several minutes. Let the candles burn out naturally. Provided your need is genuine, a windfall should be on its way.

When it arrives, say thank you to the mystic world.

[69]

A Romany saying to induce money luck is "Trinka Five."

TAROT
MONEY SPELL

The Romanies strongly believe in Tarot cards. This spell to bring money takes fourteen days to perform, fourteen green candles, and the Coins suit (fourteen cards) taken from a pack of Tarot cards.

On the night of a new moon, light a green candle. Take the Ace of Coins card from a Tarot deck and place it face up, flat on its back, behind the candle.

[70]

Sit for a few minutes looking at the candle flame, thinking about what you will do with the money you wish for. Leave the card in position and allow the candle to burn down and extinguish itself.

On the following evening, light a new candle. Place the Two of Coins card, face up, to the right of the Ace of Coins and slightly below it, to begin forming a clockwise circle of cards. Sit gazing at the flame and ponder again how you will use the money you want. Leave the card in place and the candle to extinguish itself.

On the following night perform the same sequence, using a new candle and the Three of Coins card. On the fourth evening use the Four of Coins, and continue until on the tenth night you have placed the Ten of Coins card in position and left the candle to burn down.

On the eleventh night, use the Knave of Coins card. The illustration on the card depicts a young man giving you money. Dwell on that thought as you look into the flame.

On the twelfth night, place the Knight of Coins card in position and again let the picture on the card direct your thoughts.

On the thirteenth night, use the Queen of Coins card. The Queen card depicts a woman giving you money. Again, allow your imagination to drift as you look at the card and candle flame.

On the fourteenth night, which will be a full moon, your last card will be the King of Coins. He has money in his hand and is giving it to you.

Leave the cards in position and let the candle burn out of its own accord.

The following morning, return the suit of Coins to the pack. Money should start rolling in!

Romany horse dealers use the term "lucky penny" when making transactions. The dealer returns a coin or banknote to the buyer, for luck.

WEALTHY WEEK

On a Sunday evening, burn a gold candle surrounded by piles of loose change. It is important not to count the cash. If there are so few coins you cannot help but notice, cover them with a handkerchief. Watching the candle flame, say: "Thank you for the money I have already received from the invisible world."

[72]

Leave the candle to burn down and extinguish itself. Afterward gather up the coins. You will need them for the next evening's spell.

On Monday burn a white candle in the same way, adding to the heap of coins any more you have accumulated throughout the day. Repeat words of thanks for money already received from the invisible world.

On Tuesday use a pink candle and add to the coin collection the loose change the day has brought you. Speak the magic words again.

Continue with the words and the same coins, adding daily to the pile. Use a red candle on Wednesday, a green candle on Thursday, a blue candle on Friday, and on Saturday a green candle.

Stash away your cash and reserve it for money spells. The more coins you accumulate, the greater the power of attraction. (Of course, you can also throw the coins into your purse.)

Bubbles floating on a cup of tea augur money.

money-drawing oil

3 drops wood marjoram oil

2 drops lemon oil

2 drops eucalyptus oil

Romanies roll their bills rather
than keeping them flat.
Smearing the outside bill with
Money-Drawing Oil is believed
to attract cash.

Oiling the Wheel of Fortune

The following ancient Romany formulas can be used
to enhance the vibration of your spells. They are designed
for anointing candles, coins, paper, or other objects mentioned in
this book. They should not be worn on the skin.

lucky planet oil

5 drops ylang ylang oil

3 drops clary sage oil

5 drops geranium oil

Lucky Planet Oil rubbed on an
orange candle, which is then left
to burn down, is said to encourage a lucky turn of events.

commanding oil

6 drops patchouli oil

8 drops myrrh oil

16 drops sandalwood oil

Commanding Oil is dabbed on uncounted coins, which are then placed in the light of a full moon as a statement that money is required.

compelling oil

8 drops sandalwood oil

4 drops myrrh oil

2 drops cinnamon oil

Compelling Oil is known to have been used to encourage business deals. It is smeared on a candle, which is lit the night before a negotiation. Alternatively, it is used to anoint money used in a transaction, to ensure future business with the same person.

lady luck oil

4 drops sandalwood oil

7 drops rose oil

5 drops lavender oil

Romany women are said to anoint their clothing with Lady Luck Oil, to ensure success when hawking or fortune-telling. It is also used on candles and money.

power oil

5 drops frankincense oil

2 drops cypress oil

3 drops juniper oil

Power Oil is generally used to strengthen any spell, whether it is for health, wealth, love, or happiness. A few dabs on clothing helps a person win in a situation where they feel the odds are stacked against them.

URGENT
MONEY SPELL

The Romanies say that when money is urgently needed by a certain date, this spell works wonders. One thing to remember: it must be performed at the witching hour of midnight.

Take one white votive candle to represent each $100 or $1,000 that you critically need. Stand them on a plate you often eat from.

At a quarter to midnight, sit in a room with no electric lights. Light a gold or silver, green or white candle (not one of those representing money). This is the candle that will give power to the "money" votive candles and will enable you to see what you are doing.

Now work your magic. Pray for a circle of gold light to be placed around you for protection and for a circle of blue light to be placed around you for healing.

Pick up a votive candle and light it from the main candle flame. As you do so, say that the votive you are lighting represents the $100, or $1,000, you need. Place it on the plate to begin a circle of "money" candles.

Light each votive, and say the same words for each, until the circle is complete.

Say a prayer explaining that you are not being greedy; that the money is necessary. Leave the candles to burn out of their own accord. The money should start winging its way to you.

TO WIN A BET

Light seven green candles and say:

> Abracadabra
> Abracadabr
> Abracadab
> Abracada
> Abraca
> Abrac
> Abr
> Ab
> A

Repeat seven times and extinguish the candle. Do this for seven days. When you place your bet you are more likely to win.

THE LOTTERY

The Romanies often like to gamble, and they advise using this spell for the lottery.

Light one green candle for each of the numbers to be selected. Sit quietly and ponder the flames, allowing each flame in turn to suggest a number.

Fill in the form according to the numbers that come into your head. Sprinkle the sheet with nutmeg and then snuff out the candles. Leave the form dusted with nutmeg for a day before thoroughly brushing it off.

[77]

Tradition says that if you drop money and someone else picks it up for you and puts it in your hands, it is an omen of more money to come. It is unlucky for the recipient of a gift of a purse or wallet not to receive a coin inside it.

AN INTERVIEW
DIVINATION

Although Romanies are historically and instinctively nomads, they sometimes want to stay in one place. This means they must seek work, perhaps on a farm, or find an outlet for their trade. They use the following divination to foretell whether or not they will get a job interview.

Take two acorns. One represents you, and the other the person you have applied to for a job. Place both acorns in a bowl of water. If they float side by side or touch, you will get an interview. If they float in opposite directions, you will not.

Easy Money Spells

Light a green candle. Let it burn
for five minutes, then blow it
out. Rub your hands in the smoke
and imagine money coming
to you.

On the night of the new moon, place a coin
on a windowsill with the head facing up.
When the moon is full, flip the coin so the
tails side is facing up — this encourages
money problems to diminish. Then, keeping
in harmony with the moon phases, finish
the spell by removing the coin on a new or
full moon.

When the moon is new, you can open the channels for money by using a spiral money spell. ¶ Collect as many coins as possible. Light a green candle and place it to the left side of a table. Now work only by candlelight. ¶ To the right of the candle, form the coins into a spiral shape until you have run out of change. ¶ On clean white paper, in green ink, write the amount of money that you need, and the reason. At the end of your wish add, "By the grace of God," to ensure the money comes through good fortune. ¶ Place the wish to the right of the coins and leave it there until the candle has burned down. Scoop up the coins to spend or keep. ¶ Put the paper containing the wish in your wallet or purse, where it should be kept until your wish has been fulfilled.

TO WIN A JOB

Before you go to your job interview, you will need a green candle, a banknote, and a paper clip.

Light the candle and show both sides of the banknote to the flame. Fasten the note to the back of a photograph of yourself. Blow out the candle.

Carry your photo, with the note attached, in your handbag or wallet during your interview.

[81]

Seeing a spider weave its web — specially if the web is on a window or door — is an omen of money luck.

The web must not be removed until money has arrived.

MORE WAYS
TO BRING MONEY
HOME

When the moon is new, secretly place a $10, $20, or $50 bill underneath the front doormat inside your home. It will be charged with positive energy every time someone walks over it. The greater the value of the note, the larger your returns could be. The note should only be removed when the moon is full; otherwise you will attract unexpected expense to your door.

- Plant marigolds on top of a golden-colored object. Whether they are in a pot, tub, window box, or your garden, the marigolds should be as close to your front door as possible.

- On the night of a new moon, and in moonlight, place as many bills and coins as you can muster on a windowsill. Avoid the temptation to count the money, because that limits the boundaries of expectation. The greater the amount of money, the greater you can expect your financial increase to be. Say:

> Oh beautiful moon, please radiate wealth into my life with your light.

Your financial fortune will begin to flow and show signs of fruition at the full moon. To keep money flowing, repeat the spell when you next see the crescent of the new moon appear in the sky.

Happiness

From the time the Romanies arrived in Britain in the fifteenth century, they protected themselves with a positive attitude. Whatever wasn't good wasn't worth thinking about, and they focused on their search for happiness and talismans forecasting good luck.

STONE SPELL

A stone with a hole through it is regarded as an amulet to ward off evil. It should be threaded on cord hung on or over a door, to act as an all-seeing eye.

It can also be used as a wishing stone. Wash the stone in running water to cleanse it. Write your wish, with chalk or a pen, on the stone. What you wish for is now "written in stone." Make sure your request is precise and leaves no room for loopholes.

When the sun is setting, face west and embed the stone in soil. Beside it place a piece of blue cord, blue cotton, or blue ribbon with a knot to represent your wish. Fill the hole in the stone with allspice. Sprinkle the spell with water and speak your wish while you cover it with soil.

The winds of change will bring your wish to you. Do not doubt, or think about your wish once you have buried your stone.

HORSESHOE
WISHING SPELL

Many Romanies were once blacksmiths; they used iron horseshoes in their spells for happiness, and today to find a horseshoe is still considered an omen of good luck. To find a shoe with nails in it is especially fortunate; each nail denotes a year of luck. The more nails, the more years of luck lie ahead. (Contrarians believe each nail represents a year the finder will have to wait before marrying.)

To cast a spell with a rusty horseshoe, first brush the rust off with a wire brush, so the holes are open. Light a red candle in a room with no other light. Sit in front of the candle and write seven wishes on seven small squares of paper.

Use green paper for a money wish; blue for health; pink for love; red for employment; purple or lilac for

A horseshoe nailed to a door, or over a door, is said to act as a protective amulet. It attracts good luck and defies evil to cross the threshold. Placed with the open en

friendship; yellow for spiritual concerns; orange for legal matters; brown for the home; and white for miscellaneous matters. Make sure your wishes are precise, because fuzzy ideas get fuzzy results.

Roll the squares tightly and poke them through each hole in the horseshoe. List your wishes on a separate piece of paper, numbered from one to seven, from left to right on the shoe, so that you know, at a later date, which hole holds each specific wish. Snuff out the candle.

Place the horseshoe in a shoe or boot box and hide the box away. It is important at this point to forget your wishes. Set a time in the future when you will return to check off your list and to remove the slips of paper that represent wishes come true.

pointing upward, it catches good luck and keeps it.

TO MEET
WITH SUCCESS

A Commanding Spell: This spell will place you on the threshold of success. It may also be used to increase your personal power before an important meeting.

Light a blue candle in front of a mirror. Sit at the mirror and stare into your own eyes in search of your soul.

Ask for a circle of gold light to be placed around you for protection and a circle of blue light to be placed around you for healing. Repeat your Christian name or names twenty-one times.

Then speak your wish and repeat it twenty-one times. Blow out the candle and await success.

Every morning say:
"A miracle is going to happen today.
This attracts good fortune and has a magnetic and cumulative effect.

Within a short space of time, you will receive a fantastic telephone call

THE KEY
TO HAPPINESS

The Romanies believe that it is extremely lucky to find a key. It means that you will soon be opening a door to success in love, marriage, or work, or even something very specific, such as getting a new car. No matter the form, happiness is assured.

With a key at hand, light a white candle. Visualize the metaphorical door you wish to open with the key. On a piece of paper, draw a door that will open to your wish.

Pour some candle wax on the drawing of the door and place the key in the wax, to weld the two together. Let the wax cool. Fold the paper around the key to form a neat envelope or parcel. Generously seal all the edges with more wax from the candle. Blow out the candle.

At night, toss the parcel into a fire, imagining as vividly as possible the door you are passing through. Pour your passion into the flames and send your desires heavenward. The spell has been cast. Do not dwell on your wish, because such thoughts drag it back to earth and sap its energy. Have faith. Believe in the miracle, and it will happen.

or letter, or you will meet someone who will change your life for the better.

NEEDLE SPELL

Aneedle that is accidentally dropped and then found poking upward foretells a visitor before the end of the day. The needle should be picked up and kept. As they say,

> Find a pin, pick it up,
> And all day long you'll have good luck.

To extend your luck for longer than one day, place the needle in a vase of fresh water and fresh flowers. The essence of the flowers will energize the luck in the needle, and your luck will last longer than the flowers.

When the flowers die, discard them as usual, empty the water, and put the needle in your sewing kit as a reminder of your good luck.

Divinations

rosemary divination

A sprig of rosemary can be used to
divine a yes or no answer to a
question. First, ask the question
seven times. Then pluck a leaf from
the sprig and say, "Yes." Pluck
another leaf and say, "No."
Continue alternating yes and no
with each leaf you pick, until
the sprig is bare. The last leaf you
pick reveals the answer.

hair divinations

Throw some hair into a fire.
It is said to be a sign of long life if
the hair flames up vigorously.
It is an omen of ill health if it simply
smolders away.¶ To determine
whether a person is flirtatious,
pluck a single hair from their
head. The hair should then be
stretched between the forefingers
and thumbs. The more it curls
when released, the more
flirtatious the owner.¶ Another
piece of lore: if a woman's hairpin
falls out, someone is thinking
of her.

water divination

Romany children play at
divination using water and a ston
to find the answer to a question.
¶ Holding a stone, sit in front
of a bowl of water and
ask a question, one that can be
answered with either a yes
or a no.¶ Drop the stone
into the water and carefully count
the ripples it creates. An even
number of ripples means yes;
an odd number, no.

LOVE OF
MOTHER-IN-LAW

Whether or not you're married, everyone will be happier if your partner's mother loves you. You can win your mother-in-law over by sending your love to her.

Choose a Friday evening when the moon is waxing. Take a pink candle and write your wish around it. Your wish should come from the heart. It could be something as simple as:

[*Mother-in-law's name*], love me.

Take a pin with a blue head, for healing, or a yellow head, for enlightenment. Between the beginning and end of your message, pierce the candle with the pin so that its tip emerges on the other side of the candle.

Light the candle and imagine the light of the flame warming your mother-in-law's heart. Leave the candle to burn down and extinguish itself, and salvage the pin.

Now have a tulip bulb ready, because tulips are said to heal rifts and reunite. Confirm your wish as you push the pin into the bulb. Then bury the bulb in a plant pot or garden. Your mother-in-law's love for you will grow with the bulb.

TO HAVE AN OBJECT RETURNED

These are easy remedies that will help you to regain an object that someone has failed to return.

- Pick a convenient time of day when you will be able to sit undisturbed for five minutes. Will the object back to you. If you sit wishing it back into your life, the thief will begin to feel uncomfortable, and will finally bring the missing item to you.

- Another method is to place an iron nail on a window-sill. It should be pointed north, south, west, or east, in whichever direction the person who has the object lives. Simply will the object back every time you look at the nail. When the object has been returned the nail should be buried or restored to the tool kit it came from.

- Another Romany remedy is to place a rose beside an object similar to the one that is missing. Love, symbolized by the rose, will prick someone's conscience and the object will be returned.

BIRTHDAY SPELL

It is unlucky to cry on your birthday. If you do, it is said, you'll cry all year through. The traditional birthday wish is made by blowing out candles on a birthday cake, but you can also conjure up a happy year ahead with flowers.

Write your birthday wish on a piece of paper and keep it under a vase of flowers. Or plant a seed or bulb while you think of your wish, and your wish will grow with the plant.

It is unlucky to find a knife.
The finder should not pick it up.
To drop a knife is a sign that
a man will visit;
to drop a spoon, a woman;
a fork, a fool.

TO GET ANOTHER
TO AGREE

Light a pink candle for love and a blue candle for healing on a Friday evening. Say the following incantation:

> Please [*name of person*], do think again.
> May the consequence heal my pain.
> Grant my request to me and you'll see,
> The good in your heart set me free.
> Bless you.

Snuff the candles out after casting your spell.

To find an old key is magical
It is said that the finder
will experience spiritual mysteries
and have prophetic dreams
They will become a channel of
communication between heaven
and earth.

TO MAKE FRIENDS
WITH FATE

Fate, it is said, may be influenced in your favor if you know your personal magic word.

To find it, light a white candle and sit facing south. Take a dictionary. Close your eyes and turn the book around several times so that you are unaware of which way it is facing.

Eyes closed, fan the pages until you feel compelled to stop at a certain page.

Eyes still closed, wander about the page using your forefinger until you feel inclined to pause. Open your eyes. Look at the word under your finger. If there is more than one word, pick the first that jumps out at you from the page. This is your magic word.

You can remind yourself of your magic word mentally or verbally whenever you wish to tune in to a situation, or whenever you feel you need a boost of energy. It will change the vibration around you and attract good influences.

But to break a key
　　　is an unfortunate omen:
it predicts a broken relationship.

GETTING JUSTICE

If the law has treated you unfairly, invoke this spell and justice will be done.

Take the Justice card from a Tarot deck. Now light a blue candle and place the Justice card on the right-hand side. Write your name and address on an unused piece of white or green paper and place it to the left of the candle. Romanies sometimes use their thumbprint instead of their name and address.

Light thirteen votive candles, to represent the thirteen lunar cycles of a year, and place them in a circle around the candle and card.

Say a prayer in which you ask for protection to be placed around you and your family.

Write your wish regarding the legal matter on a piece of paper. Sprinkle it with rose oil and burn it in the blue candle's flame. Place the burning paper on a saucer until it turns to ash. Leave the candles to burn out and your wish will be fulfilled.

Special Spell Dates

the first day of the month

The first day of any month offers fresh hopes and new beginnings.
One good-luck invocation is to say "Rabbits" before any other
word on the first of the month.¶ Some say "White rabbits"
three times as the last spoken words on the eve of the new month.
On waking they say "Hares" three times. This is said to ensure
a month that is blessed with good fortune.

St. Valentine's Day: February 14

By tradition many species of birds begin pairing
off at this time. The Romanies say that if
you are unattached, a bay leaf placed under
your pillow on St. Valentine's Day will induce you
to dream of the person you will marry.

Midsummer Night's Eve: June 20

To encourage good fortune, on Midsummer Night's Eve take
an orange, to represent the sun, and a lemon, which symbolizes
the moon. Press cloves (representing brown wooden nails)
into the skin of the fruit. The cloves purge any misfortune that the
first half of the year may have brought and ensure that the
second half of the year will be trouble free.¶ To entice a lover to
return, pick five roses on Midsummer Night's Eve. Bury one
under a yew tree at midnight. Place the second outside a church gate.
Put the third at a crossroads with the head pointing in the
direction of home. Place the fourth beside running water.
The fifth rose should be put under your pillow for three nights,
then buried.

Festival of the Holy Marys: May 25

St. Sara of Egypt is the Romanies' patron saint.
Throughout the eve of May 24 and during
May 25, Gypsies exalt the elements of fire
and water. From wood the men have gathered,
Gypsy women build a healthy campfire.
They cook a huge feast and gather around
the fire to exchange presents and good cheer.
¶ On May 24 many Romanies still make
a pilgrimage to attend an annual service at
the shrine of St. Sara of Egypt, in the crypt of the
church of Les Saintes Maries de la Mer in
the Île de la Camargue, Bouches-du-Rhône, France.
They carry the statue of St. Sara, who is black,
into the sea (from where she originated)
and out again.

St. Swithin's Day: July 15
If rain falls on St. Swithin's Day,
the Romanies believe,
forty days of rain will follow.

Halloween: October 31
To find, from a list of potential suitors, whom you are
most likely to marry, on Halloween night take one crab apple
to represent each suitor. Prick the initials of each candidate
into the skin of an apple. Leave the apples undisturbed in
a box for almost a year, until Old Michaelmas Day (October 11).
The most perfectly formed initials reveal the answer.
¶ (Another method is to take as many hazelnuts as you have
prospective partners. Name each nut accordingly before placing
them evenly on the front of the fire. The nut that pops the
loudest and burns most brightly says it all.)

Christmas: December 25
Some Romanies nowadays make and sell
holly wreaths. For the Christmas season,
they rent part of a wood, to cut evergreen.
The Romanies believe that a holly wreath
should always include both prickly
and smooth holly for domestic harmony.
Prickly holly alone is an omen that the man
will rule the roost in the New Year.

New Year's Eve: December 31

To divine whether you will marry in the New Year, try throwing a shoe or boot into a willow tree. If it gets caught in the branches, the answer is yes. You are allowed to throw the shoe no more than nine times because, in spells, nine symbolizes completion.

New Year Moons

A wish spoken to the first new moon of the New Year will be fulfilled. It is especially fortunate to see the new moon crescent on your right. The first full moon of the year is also said to make a wish come true it will be granted before the year is out. ¶ The first full moon of the year is also believed to be a mystical time when you can mysteriously see the face of your future partner appear in a pond that reflects the moon.

TO REMOVE
MISFORTUNE

According to the Romanies, extricating yourself or someone you care for from a streak of bad luck and misfortune is not difficult.

Take three small jars and nine garlic cloves, and a number of thorns from a white rose. Stick the thorns into the garlic cloves and place three cloves in each jar.

Each jar should be buried within sight of a church porch while you say the Lord's Prayer.

[103]

TO MAKE A WISH
COME TRUE

On the day of the new moon, write your wish on a sheet of clean paper, then light a new, white votive candle. At this point turn off any artificial lighting that may be on.

For ten minutes, enjoy the flame's glow and think about the fulfillment of your wish. Then say: "As I sleep tonight, may the divine power of spiritual love and light grant my wish." While concentrating on your wish, burn the piece of paper in the flame. Leave the votive candle to burn out.

Repeat the spell at the same time on twelve consecutive nights. If you miss a night, begin the spell from day one.

[104]

Here is another way to make a wish come true. On the night of a new moon, write your wish on a bay leaf. Simply take the bay leaf outside and look at the moon, then kiss the leaf three times and sleep with it under your pillow.

Since the bay tree is governed by the sun and ruled by Leo, this charm is particularly potent when the sun is in Leo, between July 23 and August 22.

[105]

Wish upon the first star
you see in the night sky,
on any night of the year.
Your wish will come true
if a second star appears
shortly afterward.

HOME SWEET HOME

Just as Romanies blessed and protected their *vardos*, so you can bless your new home and protect it from burglary and fire.

- Sprinkle salt around the perimeter, or plant garlic around the boundary.
- You can also pray for a circle of gold light for protection and a circle of blue light for healing to be placed around the home.
- Disruptive neighbors who upset the harmony of your home can be tamed quite simply. Place small hand mirrors on windowsills facing their home. These reflect back whatever they are sending out to you if you say, "Return to sender." If no anger is attached to your actions, your neighbors will respond to your influence without realizing why.

Weather Spells

No need to cross your fingers and hope for good
weather. According to the Romanies, you can
make the sun shine whenever you want it to.

Light a golden candle. Draw a five-inch map
of the area where you want the sun to shine.
Moving the map clockwise, circle it three
times around the candle flame, imagining the
flame is the sun.¶ Burn the map in the flame
while making your wish. You could say:

Fair weather I ask you to shine,
On this special day of mine,
I've chased the clouds away,
So the sun will shine all day.

Your special day will be filled with sunshine.

To stir up the wind to dry washing
on a line, stand with your back
to the breeze and exhale facing the
washing. To make it less windy,
inhale and blow the wind back in
the direction it is blowing from.

If rain is your desire, whipping pond
water with a hazel stick is believed to
invoke a downpour. This is known
as "water witching."

TO BREAK A STREAK
OF BAD LUCK

Go for a walk and pick up seven twigs from the ground, one to represent each day of the week. Traditionally, the twigs should be ash for Monday, beech for Tuesday, elm for Wednesday, oak for Thursday, horse chestnut for Friday, yew for Saturday, and elder for Sunday.

Take them home, snap them into pieces, and burn them in the hearth or a bonfire. Say:

> Ill luck is broken,
> As these words are spoken.

When two people coincidentally utter the same words at precisely the same moment, they should link fingers and each make a wish — the wishes will come true.

BROTHERLY
AND SISTERLY
LOVE

To draw children in a family closer, as well as to stop them from bickering, take water from a stream or river. Bring it to a boil on a fire built with fresh twigs. Write the name of each child on a bay leaf and let them simmer together in the water. Ask Venus to bless them.

Using a pin, inscribe the names of the children on a pink candle and then light the candle, so that its flame may flicker over your spell.

[110]

Take a pink, a blue, and a green ribbon. Braid them together, knot the ends, and tie a knot in the middle. The first knot represents will, the second, wisdom, and the third, activity.

Remove the pot from the fire and leave it to cool. Extract the bay leaves. Allow the candle and the fire to burn down.

In the garden or in an unused flowerpot, bury the ribbon under the bay leaves. Sprinkle ash from the fire on top, and then plant a rosebush or miniature rose on top of everything. (The rose is a potent ingredient in any love potion.)

As the rose grows, the bond between the children will be strengthened. This spell is also said to work when children from two marriages are brought together.

TO DETER
AN UNWANTED
VISITOR

To avoid being revisited by an unwanted caller, all you need is salt. Immediately after they have made their departure, sprinkle salt, which is regarded as a purifier and a protection against evil forces, on the ground where they said goodbye.

[111]

TO REMOVE
A PROBLEM

Write a problem on the sole of an old shoe. Put the shoe on, stamp on the problem three times, then take the shoe off and burn it in a fire.

Another method is to write your problem on a piece of paper. Dig a hole, place the paper inside, and bury it along with a piece of copper, a piece of iron, and some zinc.

The simplest remedy is to write your problem on a piece of paper and throw it into a fire.

FOR A LIFE
FILLED WITH
SUNSHINE

St.-John's-wort, a golden flower that smells like turpentine, is regarded as an emblem of the sun.

Light an orange candle and place a bunch of St.-John's-wort beside it. Make a wish, then hang the bunch of St.-John's-wort over an entrance door to your home. Leave the candle to extinguish itself. It will bring you your wish and ward off evil too.

[112]

Bad luck at home can be avoided by never washing blankets during the waxing May moon. According to the saying "If you wash blankets in May, you will wash a loved one away."

Epilogue

We leave the Romanies by their campfire,
where if a spark flies, they will know a surprise is on its way.
Friends of moonlight and magic, superstition and prophecy,
they are at one with the spirits alive
in every flame, tree, breeze, and stone. ¶ As they sit round
a campfire, romance and hopes of a golden future
beckon to them, and as they have for centuries,
the elders tell the young of their age-old traditions
and the spells that can bring
love, health, wealth, and happiness.

one last spell

A flickering fire can mesmerize even the most hardened cynic.
So, on a balmy summer night, when the moon is full, organize a
Romany firelight party. A good bonfire would be ideal, but with
a bit of imagination even a spluttering barbecue will do.

In a dark corner of the garden, place a candlelit table for the
local fortune-teller. Find a violinist friend to improvise the fiddling
of exciting, passionate, romantic Zingari tunes. (You could cheat
by buying discs of Gypsy music and hiding the CD player behind a
bush. In the wild dancing that follows, nobody will complain.)

As the fire glows and flickers, pour a glass or two of rich Gypsy
wine, such as Hungarian Bull's Blood, and you will cast a Romany
spell over everyone.

As the Romanies say today: "The Tatcho drom to be a jin-
neypenmengro is to dik to shoon and to rig drey zi" — The true
way to be a wise man is to see, to hear, and to bear in mind.

Gillian Kemp is a freelance writer and astrologer. As a journalist she met Olive Cox, the last Romany girl in Britain to be born, marry, and bear her own children in a horse-drawn caravan.

Her horoscope columns appear regularly in British magazines, and she is a frequent contributor to cable television. She is about to publish her second book, *Tea Leaves, Herbs, and Flowers: Fortune-telling the Gypsy Way.* Gillian Kemp also entertains as a clairvoyant medium at parties in top hotels and restaurants.

She lives in England with her beloved dog, Daisy May.

Library of Congress Cataloging-in-Publication Data
Kemp, Gillian.
   [Romany good spell book]
   The good spell book : love charms, magical cures, and other practical sorcery / Gillian Kemp. — 1st U.S. ed.
      p.   cm.
   Originally published : The Romany good spell book. London : Cassell Group, 1997.
   ISBN 0–316–48839–9
   1. Magic, Gypsy.   I. Title.
BF1622.G8K45 1999
133. 4'4'08991497 — dc21   98–8513

10 9 8 7   Q–KP
BOOK DESIGN BY JULIA SEDYKH
Printed in the United States of America